A GUIDING LIGHT WORKBOOK

Alcoholics Anonymous
12 Steps Guide

By Dale Preston

Table of Contents

The 12 Steps of AA

1. We admitted we were powerless over alcohol — that our lives had become unmanageable.
2. Came to believe that a Power greater than ourselves could restore us to sanity.
3. Made a decision to turn our will and our lives over to the care of God as we understood Him.
4. Made a searching and fearless moral inventory of ourselves.
5. Admitted to God, to ourselves, and to another human being the exact nature of our wrongs.
6. Were entirely ready to have God remove all these defects of character.
7. Humbly asked Him to remove our shortcomings.
8. Made a list of all persons we had harmed, and became willing to make amends to them all.
9. Made direct amends to such people wherever possible, except when to do so would injure them or others.
10. Continued to take personal inventory and when we were wrong promptly admitted it.
11. Sought through prayer and meditation to improve our conscious contact with God as we understood Him, praying only for knowledge of His will for us and the power to carry that out.
12. Having had a spiritual awakening as the result of these Steps, we tried to carry this message to alcoholics, and to practice these principles in all our affairs.

Step 1

We admitted we were powerless over alcohol, that our lives had become unmanageable.[1]

Under the lash of alcoholism, we are driven to A.A., and there we discover the fatal nature of our situation. Then, and only then, do we become as open-minded to conviction and as willing to listen as the dying can be. We stand ready to do anything which will lift the merciless obsession from us.[2]

Have you admitted you are NOT like other people who can drink?

☐Yes   ☐No

Explain your answer: Why?

_____

_____

_____

_____

_____

_____

_____

_____

---

[1] The Twelve Steps
[2] 12 and 12, Page 24

_____

_____

_____

_____

_____

_____

_____

_____

_____

_____

_____

_____

_____

What is the great obsession of every ABNORMAL drinker?[3]

_____

_____

_____

_____

_____

_____

_____

_____

_____

_____

_____

_____

---

[3] Preston, D., Page 88

_____

_____

_____

_____

_____

_____

_____

_____

_____

_____

_____

_____

What does it mean to be POWERLESS?

Total surrender

_____

_____

_____

_____

_____

_____

_____

_____

_____

_____

_____

_____

_____

_____

_____

_____

_____

_____

_____

_____

_____

_____

_____

_____

What are some examples of how your life has become UNMANAGEABLE?

I had to borrow money to support my drinking

_____

_____

_____

_____

_____

_____

_____

_____

_____

_____

_____

Step 2

Came to believe that a power greater than ourselves could restore us to sanity.[4]

I was progressing to step two in my recovery after I fully embraced and accepted the first step. Once I acknowledged that my life was unmanageable and insane, I moved on to step two. I acknowledged the insanity in my life and believed in the guiding presence of my higher power, knowing that it could bring me back to sanity.[5]

What is your definition of INSANITY?[6]

_____

_____

_____

_____

_____

_____

_____

_____

---

[4] The Twelve Steps
[5] Preston, D., Page 93
[6] Preston, D., Page 88

What are some examples of how your life became INSANE?

I thought that the next time I drank I wouldn't end up in a black-out

_____

_____

_____

_____

_____

_____

_____

_____

_____

_____

_____

_____

_____

_____

_____

_____

_____

_____

_____

_____

_____

_____

_____

_____

_____

_____

Do you believe in a power greater than yourself?

☐Yes ☐No

Explain your answer: Why?

_____

_____

_____

_____

_____

_____

_____

_____

_____

_____

_____

_____

_____

_____

_____

_____

_____

_____

_____

_____

_____

_____

_____

_____

What are some examples of how a power greater than yourself can restore you to sanity?

By helping me see the truth

_____

_____

_____

_____

_____

_____

_____

_____

_____

_____

_____

Step 3

Made a decision to turn our will and our lives over to the care of God as we understood him.[7]

Steps one through three were decision steps. If you have three frogs on a log and one of them decides to jump off, how many frogs are left on the log? The answer is three, because the one frog only decided to jump off; it never actually jumped off. Once I completed steps one and two, it was easy for me to take the third step.

The rest of the twelve steps were action steps. You will not find the word "decision" anywhere else in the steps. They require us to take action.[8]

Describe GOD, as you understand him:

I believe God is Omniscient, Omnipotent, Omnipresent, All-loving, and All-forgiving.

_____

_____

_____

_____

_____

_____

_____

_____

---

[7] The Twelve Steps
[8] Preston D., Page 93

Dose your understanding of God include a LOVING and CARING God?

☐Yes ☐No

Explain your answer: Why?

_____

_____

_____

_____

_____

_____

_____

_____

_____

_____

Are you ready to turn your WILL and LIFE over to his care?

☐Yes ☐No

Explain your answer: Why?

_____

_____

_____

_____

_____

_____

_____

_____

_____

_____

_____

_____

_____

_____

_____

_____

_____

_____

_____

_____

_____

_____

_____

_____

What are some examples of how you can turn your will and life over to him?

By setting aside time every morning for prayer. "God, I offer myself to Thee – to build with me and to do with me as Tho wilt. Relieve me of the bondage of self, that I may better do Thy will. Take away my difficulties, that victory over them may bear witness to those I would help of Thy Power, Thy Love, and Thy Way of life. May I do Thy will always!"[9]

_____

_____

_____

_____

_____

_____

_____

_____

_____

_____

[9] The Big Book, Page 63.

Step 4

Made a searching and fearless moral inventory of ourselves.[10]

Therefore, thoroughness ought to be the watchword when taking inventory. In this connection, it is wise to write out our questions and answers. It will be an aid to clear thinking and honest appraisal. It will be the first tangible evidence of our complete willingness to move forward.[11]

What does it mean to you to be SEARCHING and FEARLESS?[12]

_____

_____

_____

_____

_____

_____

_____

_____

---

[10] The Twelve Steps
[11] 12 and 12, Page 54
[12] Preston, D., Page 89

_____

_____

_____

_____

_____

_____

_____

_____

_____

_____

_____

_____

Make a list of your POSITIVE moral character traits:

I am a hard worker	1.
2.	3.
4.	5.
6.	7.
8.	9.
10.	11.
12.	13.
14.	15.
16.	17.
18.	19.
20.	21.
22.	23.
24.	25.
26.	27.
28.	29.

Make a list of your NEGATIVE moral character traits:

Telling lies	1.
2.	3.
4.	5.
6.	7.
8.	9.
10.	11.
12.	13.
14.	15.
16.	17.
18.	19.
20.	21.
22.	23.
24.	25.
26.	27.
28.	29.

Make a list of your RESENTMENTS, INJURIES, AND AFFECTS:

I'M RESENTFUL AT: (People, institutions, or principles)	THE CAUSE	AFFECTS MY:
My employer	They fired me	☒ Self-esteem ☐ Sex-Relations ☒ Security ☒ Personal Pride ☐ Relationships
1.		☐ Self-esteem ☐ Sex-Relations ☐ Security ☐ Personal Pride ☐ Relationships
2.		☐ Self-esteem ☐ Sex-Relations ☐ Security ☐ Personal Pride ☐ Relationships
3.		☐ Self-esteem ☐ Sex-Relations ☐ Security ☐ Personal Pride ☐ Relationships
4.		☐ Self-esteem ☐ Sex-Relations ☐ Security ☐ Personal Pride ☐ Relationships
5.		☐ Self-esteem ☐ Sex-Relations ☐ Security ☐ Personal Pride ☐ Relationships
6.		☐ Self-esteem ☐ Sex-Relations ☐ Security ☐ Personal Pride ☐ Relationships
7.		☐ Self-esteem ☐ Sex-Relations ☐ Security ☐ Personal Pride ☐ Relationships
8.		☐ Self-esteem ☐ Sex-Relations ☐ Security ☐ Personal Pride ☐ Relationships

I'M RESENTFUL AT: (People, institutions, or principles)	THE CAUSE	AFFECTS MY:
9.		☐ Self-esteem ☐ Sex-Relations ☐ Security ☐ Personal Pride ☐ Relationships
10.		☐ Self-esteem ☐ Sex-Relations ☐ Security ☐ Personal Pride ☐ Relationships
11.		☐ Self-esteem ☐ Sex-Relations ☐ Security ☐ Personal Pride ☐ Relationships
12.		☐ Self-esteem ☐ Sex-Relations ☐ Security ☐ Personal Pride ☐ Relationships
13.		☐ Self-esteem ☐ Sex-Relations ☐ Security ☐ Personal Pride ☐ Relationships
14.		☐ Self-esteem ☐ Sex-Relations ☐ Security ☐ Personal Pride ☐ Relationships
15.		☐ Self-esteem ☐ Sex-Relations ☐ Security ☐ Personal Pride ☐ Relationships
16.		☐ Self-esteem ☐ Sex-Relations ☐ Security ☐ Personal Pride ☐ Relationships
17.		☐ Self-esteem ☐ Sex-Relations ☐ Security ☐ Personal Pride ☐ Relationships
18.		☐ Self-esteem ☐ Sex-Relations ☐ Security ☐ Personal Pride ☐ Relationships

Step 5

Admitted to God, to ourselves, and to another human being the exact nature of our wrongs.[13]

This feeling of being at one with God and man, this emerging from isolation through the open and honest sharing of our terrible burden of guilt, brings us to a resting place where we may prepare ourselves for the following Steps toward a full and meaningful sobriety.[14]

What was YOUR PART in your resentments?

MY RESENTMENTS: (From Step Four)	MY WRONGDOING:
I didn't go to community service and was arrested on a bench warrant	*My own failure*
1.	
2.	
3.	
4.	
5.	
6.	
7.	
8.	
9.	

---

[13] The Twelve Steps
[14] 12 and 12, Page 62

MY RESENTMENTS: (From Step Four)	MY WRONGDOING:
10.	
11.	
12.	
13.	
14.	
15.	
16.	
17.	
18.	
19.	
20.	
21.	
22.	
23.	
24.	
25.	

What was the EXACT NATURE of your wrongs?

I gave up trying to sign up for community service

_____

_____

_____

_____

_____

_____

_____

_____

_____

_____

_____

_____

Make a list of people you can TRUST to share this with?

1. _____

2. _____

3. _____

4. _____

5. _____

6. _____

7. _____

8. _____

9. _____

10. _____

11. _____

12. _____

13. _____

14. _____

_____

Are you ready to admit to God, yourself and to another human being the exact nature of your wrongs?

☐Yes ☐No

Explain your answer: Why?

_____

_____

_____

_____

_____

_____

_____

_____

_____

_____

_____

Step 6

Were entirely ready to have God remove all these defects of character.[15]

"THIS is the Step that separates the men from the boys." So declares a well-loved clergyman who happens to be one of A.A.'s greatest friends. He goes on to explain that any person capable of enough willingness and honesty to try repeatedly Step Six on all his faults— without any reservations whatever—has indeed come a long way spiritually, and is therefore entitled to be called a man who is sincerely trying to grow in the image and likeness of his own Creator.[16]

Are there any DEFECTS OF CHARACTER you missed in steps four and five, or still have?

☐Yes ☐No

My anger, selfishness, fear, and self-pity

1. _____

2. _____

3. _____

4. _____

5. _____

6. _____

7. _____

8. _____

_____

[15] The Twelve Steps
[16] 12 and 12, Page 63

9. _____

10. _____

11. _____

12. _____

13. _____

14. _____

15. _____

16. _____

17. _____

18. _____

19. _____

20. _____

21. _____

22. _____

23. _____

Are you ready to have God remove ALL these defects of character?

☐Yes ☐No

Explain your answer: Why?

_____

_____

_____

_____

_____

_____

_____

_____

_____

_____

_____

Step 7

Humbly asked him to remove our shortcomings.[17]

The chief activator of our defects has been self-centered fear—primarily fear that we would lose something we already possessed or would fail to get something we demanded. Living upon a basis of unsatisfied demands, we were in a state of continual disturbance and frustration.[18]

Are there any SHORTCOMINGS you missed in step six, or still have?

☐Yes ☐No

My selfishness

1. _____

2. _____

3. _____

4. _____

5. _____

6. _____

7. _____

8. _____

9. _____

---

[17] The Twelve Steps
[18] 12 and 12, Page 76

10. _____

11. _____

12. _____

13. _____

14. _____

15. _____

16. _____

17. _____

18. _____

19. _____

20. _____

21. _____

22. _____

23. _____

_____

Are you ready to ASK GOD to remove your shortcomings?

☐Yes ☐No

Explain your answer: Why?

_____

_____

_____

_____

_____

_____

_____

_____

_____

_____

_____

Step 8

Made a list of all persons we had harmed and became willing to make amends to them all.[19]

Here we go with another action step. Again, I had to put pen to paper and make a list of everyone I have harmed. When making my list, I needed to be humble and honest with myself, asking if anyone had been harmed by my actions. I needed to list my employer because I could not give 100 percent effort to my work when I was under the influence. Another person who I harmed was my ex-wife. I harmed her by spending my resources on drugs and alcohol instead of supporting her. The list goes on and on, and yours will too.[20]

Persons you have harmed	What is the nature of your harm	Are you willing to make amends?
My Ex	*Failed to pay for car insurance*	☒Yes ☐No
1.		☐Yes ☐No
2.		☐Yes ☐No
3.		☐Yes ☐No
4.		☐Yes ☐No
5.		☐Yes ☐No
6.		☐Yes ☐No
7.		☐Yes ☐No
8.		☐Yes ☐No
9.		☐Yes ☐No
10.		☐Yes ☐No
11.		☐Yes ☐No
12.		☐Yes ☐No

[19] The Twelve Steps
[20] Preston D., Page 95

Persons you have harmed	What is the nature of your harm	Are you willing to make amends?
13.		☐Yes ☐No
14.		☐Yes ☐No
15.		☐Yes ☐No
16.		☐Yes ☐No
17.		☐Yes ☐No
18.		☐Yes ☐No
19.		☐Yes ☐No
20.		☐Yes ☐No
21.		☐Yes ☐No
22.		☐Yes ☐No
23.		☐Yes ☐No
24.		☐Yes ☐No
25.		☐Yes ☐No
26.		☐Yes ☐No
27.		☐Yes ☐No
28.		☐Yes ☐No
29.		☐Yes ☐No
30.		☐Yes ☐No
31.		☐Yes ☐No
32.		☐Yes ☐No
33.		☐Yes ☐No

Step 9

Made direct amends to such people wherever possible, except when to do so would injure them or others.[21]

Most misunderstandings in this step relate to the second half, "except when to do so would injure them or others." Most people ignore this half of the step and boldly go forth with their amends. This could have severe consequences if we were not careful. We need to be honest with ourselves when taking this step. Were we making amends to make ourselves look good, or could it be hurtful in the process? Hurtful to them or others? And "others" includes us.[22]

Are you ready to make DIRECT AMENDS to such people?

☐Yes ☐No

Persons you are making amends to:	How do you plan to make these direct amends?	Would this amends injure them, yourself or others?
My Ex	*Tell her I'm sorry, pay for damages*	☒Yes ☐No
1.		☐Yes ☐No
2.		☐Yes ☐No
3.		☐Yes ☐No
4.		☐Yes ☐No
5.		☐Yes ☐No
6.		☐Yes ☐No
7.		☐Yes ☐No
8.		☐Yes ☐No
9.		☐Yes ☐No

---

[21] The Twelve Steps
[22] Preston D., Page 95, 96

Persons you are making amends to:	How do you plan to make these direct amends?	Would this amends injure them, yourself or others?
10.		☐ Yes ☐ No
11.		☐ Yes ☐ No
12.		☐ Yes ☐ No
13.		☐ Yes ☐ No
14.		☐ Yes ☐ No
15.		☐ Yes ☐ No
16.		☐ Yes ☐ No
17.		☐ Yes ☐ No
18.		☐ Yes ☐ No
19.		☐ Yes ☐ No
20.		☐ Yes ☐ No
21.		☐ Yes ☐ No
22.		☐ Yes ☐ No
23.		☐ Yes ☐ No
24.		☐ Yes ☐ No
25.		☐ Yes ☐ No
26.		☐ Yes ☐ No
27.		☐ Yes ☐ No
28.		☐ Yes ☐ No

Step 10

Continued to take personal inventory and when we were wrong promptly admitted it.[23]

AS we work the first nine Steps, we prepare ourselves for the adventure of a new life. But when we approach Step Ten we commence to put our A.A. way of living to practical use, day by day, in fair weather or foul. Then comes the acid test: can we stay sober, keep in emotional balance, and live to good purpose under all conditions?[24]

Is there anything in your PERSONAL INVENTORY where you were wrong?

I cursed at someone today. I need to apologize.

_____

_____

_____

_____

_____

_____

_____

_____

---

[23] The Twelve Steps
[24] 12 and 12, Page 88

Are you willing to ADMIT you were WRONG?

☐Yes ☐No

Explain your answer: Why?

_____

_____

_____

_____

_____

_____

_____

_____

_____

_____

_____

_____

_____

_____

_____

_____

_____

_____

_____

_____

_____

_____

_____

Step 11

Sought through prayer and meditation to improve our conscious contact with God as we understood him, praying only for knowledge of his will for us and the power to carry that out.[25]

Of all the steps, I use this one the most. Every day, I ask God what His will is for me and to give me the power to carry that out. I love the simplicity of this step, how it reminds us to only pray for one thing and nothing else: that is His will for us.[26]

As far as you know, what is GODS WILL for you?

To be a good human being

_____

_____

_____

_____

_____

_____

_____

---

[25] The Twelve Steps
[26] Preston, D., Page 97

Are you ready to ask him for the POWER to carry that out?

☐Yes ☐No

Explain your answer: Why?

_____

_____

_____

_____

_____

_____

_____

_____

_____

_____

_____

_____

_____

_____

_____

_____

_____

_____

_____

_____

_____

_____

_____

Are you ready to CARRY that out?

☐Yes ☐No

Explain your answer: Why?

_____

_____

_____

_____

_____

_____

_____

_____

_____

_____

_____

Step 12

Having had a spiritual awakening as a result of these steps, we tried to carry this message to alcoholics, and to practice these principles in all our affairs[27].

When we practice the twelfth step, we learn to pass this message on to others and live the spirit of these steps in every aspect of our lives.

We had the honor and privilege of taking AA with us into a large prison in California. We shared our stories and listened to inmates talk about theirs. By God's grace, I never had to go through what they had to endure; Being locked up for years on end and knowing you will not be let out for years to come. I am fortunate to have only spent a few weeks in jail.[28]

What does a SPIRITUAL AWAKENING[29] mean to you?

_____

_____

_____

_____

_____

_____

_____

[27] The Twelve Steps
[28] Preston, D. Page 97
[29] Preston, D. Page 93

Have you had this spiritual awakening?

☐Yes   ☐No

Explain your answer:

_____

_____

_____

_____

_____

_____

_____

_____

_____

_____

_____

How can you CARRY THIS MESSAGE to other alcoholics?

Empty the trash, make coffee, volunteer for service in my home group

_____

_____

_____

_____

_____

_____

_____

_____

_____

_____

_____

_____

_____

_____

_____

_____

_____

_____

_____

_____

_____

_____

_____

_____

How can you PRACTICE THESE PRINCIPLES in all your affairs?

Continue to pray, go to meetings, apply these principles at home and at work

_____

_____

_____

_____

_____

_____

_____

_____

_____

_____

_____

Feedback

We'd love to hear from you!

Thanks for choosing A 'Guiding Light's Workbook' to aid in your recovery journey. I am confident that with your help we can achieve great things together! By leaving a review you create a better experience for yourself and other potential customers just like you.

Please help us keep up with your needs and serve you and others better. You can share your thoughts at Amazon by going to your recent orders page, selecting 'A Guiding Light's Workbook' order, and selecting "Write a product review."

Thank you so much for being a valuable customer. If you have any questions or feedback you would like to communicate directly, logon to www.AGuidingLight.Store and select "Contact Us."

Thank you again for choosing A Guiding Light's Products.

Our Mission

Our mission is to offer guidance-inspired products to individuals all across the globe who are eager to enhance their lives, surroundings, and experiences. Our team is dedicated to continuously improving our products with the help of valuable customer interactions and feedback. We truly appreciate anything that can contribute to our mission of positively impacting others' lives by increasing their self-awareness, their connection to their environment, and their sense of direction. Together, we can make a difference!

Resources

Alcoholics Anonymous Hotline
(866) 210-1303

Alcoholics Anonymous
https://www.aa.org/

For a list of AA meetings
https://www.aa.org/meeting-guide-app

Narcotics Anonymous Hotline
(212) 929-6262

Narcotics Anonymous
https://www.na.org/

For a list of NA meetings
https://www.na.org/meetingsearch/

National Sexual Assault Hotline
(800) 656-4673

National Sexual Assault Resources
https://www.rainn.org/resources

Child Abuse Hotline
(800) 342-3720

Coalition for the Homeless Crisis Intervention Hotline
(888) 358-2384

Coalition for the Homeless General
(212) 776-2000

Safe Horizon Crime Victim Hotline
(212) 577-7777

Police Sex Crime Unit
(212) 267-7273

Safe Horizon Rape Crisis Hotline
(212) 227-3000

Suicide & Crisis Lifeline
988

Veterans Crisis Line
(800) 273-8255

References

12 and 12, The 12 Steps and 12 Traditions. (2021). New York: World Services Inc.

Preston, D. (2023). Adendum: The twelve steps. In *A Guiding Light: Navigating abuse, alcoholism and addiction* (pp. 88-93).

The Twelve Steps. (2001). In *Alcoholics Anonymous* (p. 59). New York: ALCOHOLICS ANONYMOUS WORLD SERVICES, INC.

Wilson, B. (2001). *The Big Book Alcoholics Anonymous.* New York: World Services Inc.

Made in United States
Troutdale, OR
02/25/2024

17892531R00042